Praise for

WHEN YOU SEE MY MOTHER,
ASK HER TO DANCE

"As a tireless champion of social activism, Joan Baez has never shied away from candor, no matter how difficult. Yet, here, in her first collection of poetry, we find perhaps her most personal revelations. Baez wraps her arms around the complexities of life: she writes from both bliss and grief; she embraces both the whimsical and the profound; she confronts the struggle to let go of the dichotomy black-and-white and revel in the gray. Baez's poetry shows us that life itself means accepting both the lightness and the darkness."
—RICHARD BLANCO, author of
Homeland of My Body

"Joan's ideas and musings ricochet from the profound and humanly factual to the observant and slyly humorous. Her words can be both poignantly executed and captivating in a colorful closeness that pin-points the chinks in our armor that mirror all facets of the world we inhabit. A National treasure she is indeed."
—BERNIE TAUPIN, author of
Scattershot: Life, Music, Elton, and Me

"In these courageous and soul-searching poems, Joan Baez reveals the joy and sorrow of a life lived fully. Her deceptively simple and elegant verses resonate with profound insight into what it means to be alive, looking Janus-like from past to present. Beautiful."
—GABRIEL BYRNE, author of
Walking with Ghosts

"The artist's urgency to account for 'talents' (see Matthew 25: 14-30), to complete the record and reckoning, informs this sumptuous debut collection of poems. To her work in song, on canvas, in advocacy for the human causes, this work in words claims its place among Ms. Baez's free-range creations. Brava, is the thing I say, and write on!"
—THOMAS LYNCH, author of
Bone Rosary: New & Selected Poems

WHEN YOU SEE MY MOTHER,
ASK HER TO DANCE

WHEN YOU SEE MY MOTHER, ASK HER TO DANCE

Poems

Joan Baez

Boston

GODINE

Published in 2024 by
GODINE
Boston, Massachusetts

Cover Photo Joan Baez backstage at the Newport Folk Festival in July
1965. Photo by David Gahr. Newport Festivals Foundation/Premium
Archive via Getty Images.

LIBRARY OF CONGRESS CATALOGING-IN-PUBLICATION DATA
Names: Baez, Joan, author.
Title: When you see my mother, ask her to dance : poems / Joan Baez.
Other titles: When you see my mother, ask her to dance (Compilation)
Description: Boston : Godine, 2024.
Identifiers: LCCN 2023050836 (print) | LCCN 2023050837 (ebook) | ISBN
    9781567928013 (hardback) | ISBN 9781567928020 (ebook)
Subjects: LCSH: Baez, Joan—Poetry. | LCGFT: Autobiographical poetry.
Classification: LCC PS3602.A387 W48 2024 (print) | LCC PS3602.A387
    (ebook) | DDC 811/.6—dc23/eng/20231106
LC record available at https://lccn.loc.gov/2023050836
LC ebook record available at https://lccn.loc.gov/2023050837

First Printing, 2024
Printed in the United States of America

To Jasmine
and to the future

✑ CONTENTS ✑

III.

POETRY AND ME

An Author's Note

What do I want to say to you who has, by chance or design, picked up this little book?

That it is filled with unschooled techniques, undisciplined phrasing, haphazard thoughts, and much channeling from sources residing within me and sources unknown. It is filled with mystery and clarity, fire and darkness, blunders and eurekas, deities and demons. Some thoughts and images arrived on lightning, some crept up from deep below the damp sod.

Early drafts of many poems in this book were written between 1991 and 1997. During that time, I wrote obsessively. I was, in part, writing for many little authors, or they for me. In 1990 I began therapy that led to a diagnosis of dissociative identity disorder. That's clinical-speak for developing multiple personalities as a way of coping with long-term trauma. Some of the poems in this collection are heavily influenced by, or in effect written by, some of the inner authors. Together, we were swept up effortlessly in a tidal wave of imagery and words, and discovered what we already knew: poetry is like love—it can't be forced. All we could do was await its birth and celebrate its arrival.

I.

GOODBYE TO THE BLACK AND WHITE BALL

I used to think the alternative to black and white
must be gray. To avoid living a dull life,
I dressed in black and white,
I thought in black and white—
not just *good* or *bad*, mind you,
but *perfect* or *damned*
gifted or *worthless*
ethereal or *demonic*
emblazoned or *cast out.*

I scoffed at anything average
and avoided middle ground—
you know, The Gray Area.
As a result, I let slip most of my life.

I was chronically anxious, insomniac,
promiscuous, multiphobic, depressed,
hypervigilant, and, luckily, immensely talented.

I had antennae that could turn corners ahead of me,
protect me from the mortal danger of, say,
eating dinner in a restaurant
or making a new friend—
you know, The Gray Area.

When I was half a century old, I tore off the antennae
and turned my life over
to a power greater than myself—
which by that point could have been
a toothpick.

I pitched myself into a sea of memories
and headed blindly like a hoodwinked shark
for the marrow of the inner core me;
I pictured pustules of venom but
my therapist suggested it might be diamonds.

For months, I thrashed about,
recording dreams, grasping for clues,
fighting for my life and the life of my son.
When I came up for air from my flailing,
I began to see shards of color.

Slowly, I began to see my life was
sanctified, matchless,
and I would trade it for no other.
I should not have been shocked to find that
a diamond was in fact the core of me.

I continued to scrape off tenacious parasites.
I discovered that sorrow is an ocean,
fury is blue, pain is my companion,
but love had not been smashed to bits
so badly as to not be mendable,
like a gypsy violin
crushed beneath a Nazi boot.

I needed patience and an artisan.
My therapists became my artisans.

People around me
unearthed the gems I had been promised

and held my heart
in their cradling hands
as I split up into a hundred pieces,
a hundred bright souls
sorting out their places in a dazzling necklace
taking in and reflecting sunlight,
working to mend me,
to help me survive my deliverance
and transcend my survival.

II.

THE FIELD

There is a freshness in the grass, a lushness in the miner's lettuce, a re-greening of the oak branches after sullen winter, a sweetness in the wind that trumpets the end of the rains and heralds the true spring.

KINDERGARTEN

It's quiet out here except for the mockingbird, kids playing at the far end of the schoolyard, and the thumping of my heart. Sourgrass and miner's lettuce grow where I sit at the foot of the redwoods. After school, the kids climb the huge oak trees and scare their parents half to death. I do not climb; I am a coward who stays close to the ground.

I'm dressed in my overalls because the boys will pull my skirt up in kindergarten and the teachers will just say, "Stand up for yourself!" but I cannot. The teachers don't protect me for a minute; I think they should, as they are so big. My mind wanders off. It's nice to be dreamy and sleepy where I squat, brushing away gnats and listening to the voices of the little kids playing on the jungle gym.

I feel sad for the she-she boy who's like a girl, because everyone hates him and they push him. I'm the only one who'll play with him, and he isn't much fun. He's very pale and sad and has pretty eyes. He is scared of the Saint Bernard who lives on the grounds, who is as big as a truck and always wants to play. Yesterday he came running toward me wagging his tail and I screamed and toppled over and rolled down the slope and wet my pants.

I love the older boys and want to feel their arms. I think that I'm so small they won't even notice if I get near and reach out and touch them while they stand in the dirt on the big diamond, trading things.

The shady patch here is mossy with a few sun mottles.

My heart within me thumps away and I gaze through sleepy eyes at the long grass and buttercups and weeds with the tiny orange flowers and I know that we are different and separate from everything, my heart and I, and being this way makes us very, very tired. I feel sure there is another me with a thumping heart somewhere, lonely and leaning, just like this, against a tree.

GROUNDED

"You're grounded!" growled the father
 at the smiling, spinning daughter.

"Grounded!?" she thought, stopping in midair.

"How great! I went to Aikido, Tai Chi, Chi Gong,
 and Nepal trying to get grounded . . . and nothing doing!

Then poof, just like that,
 Daddy tells me I'm grounded!"

She smiled happily,
and went on spinning.

BAA BAA

I remember
standing offstage
clinging to the curtain
and gazing at a woman
across in the opposite wing
who was waving her hand
frantically

and looking desperate.

I stared spellbound
at her arm cutting
designs in the air
and then waving
in a beckoning motion.

She also looked very angry.

As it turns out,
she was the drama coach
there at the children's community center

and she was trying to
cue on Little Bo-Peep's
lost sheep,

which was me
all sweaty
in my woolen costume
with cotton balls glued on,

and so transfixed was I
that I missed my chance forever
to walk to center stage on all fours
and moan, "Baa Baa."

LILY

Lily lived in a farmhouse at the edge of town
where the air smelled of a pea factory just down the road,
and the alfalfa field just this side of it.
Lily had black eyes and clear skin like white hand soap,
a mean dad,
a hayloft,
chickens,
and four older brothers who made me dream.

Lily and I were eight years old and best friends.
Her lower jaw worked in a fascinating way when she talked
in her soft voice
and yodeled for me
in the echoey bathroom
of the one room schoolhouse.

Lily's family was Mennonite,
so she had long braids like rope,
which she hated.

Lily ran off and got married as soon as she turned sixteen.
Decades later, I stopped in Buffalo and saw her and
her kids.
She had hair so short
the back of her neck was shaved around the nape.
She gave me a card and laughed and said she had
a little business
making silk roses.
She was the same sweet Lily.
She even yodeled for me.

She was the same sweet, beautiful Lily who gave me
a chicken leg
forty years earlier
when school let out
and my family had to move west,
so I took it with me
in a paper sack
for the long drive
and when I got homesick
I pulled it out and yanked on the tendons to make the
claws bend.
But it began to stink
and I had to throw it away in the desert
and I cried
because as it went flying out the car window
a big blast of air came in
and hit me in the face
and I thought I smelled the pea factory
and the alfalfa field
and the dusty hay
and I thought I saw Lily's clear skin and black eyes,
and her four handsome brothers
thundering alongside our station wagon
bareback on ponies,
and they kidnapped me and took me to the mountains,
where Lily was waiting,
her long hair hanging loose in the wind,
The Princess of the Lakes
with a deerskin dress for me,
The Daughter of the Moon,
come home.

MOVING

The move.
The new house.

Unknown hallways.
Unfamiliar smells.

Unsettling fear.
"We'll have to paint this room here."

The people before us left a bureau behind,
a mastodon my mother calls it.

Can you imagine?
A prehistoric bureau?

Mom,
I miss Lily and her farm,

so many miles away over the mountains.
Mom,

we want to go investigate
and snoop into all the stuff the people abandoned.

My wildest dream is to find a
necklace

tucked in the musky old mastodon
in the too-dark hallway

at the foot of the stairs,
someone's priceless treasure

forgotten, left behind
in the hollow black drawer.

Broken clasp or not,
it would belong to me:

my staked claim
in the new house.

MY BEAUTIFUL YOUNG MOM

My beautiful young mom,
in her homemade flower print dress
with puffed sleeves
a white collar
and a waistband
that ends in a pretty bow at the back,
puts on an apron
and cleans the boarding house top to toe.

She cooks meals for ten people,
buys fish from the fish truck on Thursdays,
keeps the budget
in an accordion shaped folder:

    So much for household utilities
    So much for groceries
    So much for gas
    And not so much for new stockings.

She tends to us and all our small wants.

When she finally sits down
for a cigarette break,
she dreams of a lighter load.
She makes smoke rings for us
and we poke our fingers through them,
then beg her to make tiny spit bubbles
under her tongue
and blow them into the air.

She obliges.

For the moment the struggle stops,
or is tamped down . . .
She puts on a record of Björling.
His silvery tearful voice fills her soul,
and the screeching gulls cease to feast
upon her beautiful young heart.
Perhaps this glorious moment
can last forever.

MAYBE

How idiotic, sixteen years old and never been kissed, well not really maybe tonight, I like the way this Johnny smells and the feel of his arms his collar turned up and maybe he likes me too in the turquoise darkness of his truck, he slows down on the dead streets of my neighborhood, maybe my mother and father are asleep maybe the lights will be out so Johnny turns off the engine a half a block from the house, maybe we will glide to just under the streetlamp or just past it to the black shadows of the neighbor's magnolia tree Johnny knows, maybe I should say something maybe I should duck my head and maybe maybe I won't appear too stupid or un-appealing, maybe I have the Indian princess look especially here in the dim glow of the light from the radio that he's clicking off now so maybe, oops it's all dark, maybe it's time to get out *Thanks, it was really nice, maybe Friday, maybe,* oh stop me please don't let me go so quickly, maybe you know exactly how I feel, so flustered there's your arm may-be you love me in some way maybe I love you, well maybe I love your mouth in the shadows and the smell of roses from my mother's little garden, my mother's little garden along the edge of our lawn, your mouth maybe it should fit on mine like my drawings of couples kissing, what happens do I tilt my head like this, oh oh I thought it would be drier I have to go now my parents will be angry, maybe they're right maybe you're not supposed to do what I just did, christ it was only a kiss in the dark, I am a fool maybe I'll look different in the light in the mirror, maybe he thinks I'm an idiot, maybe I am

KISSING YOU

I'm not sorry
for kissing you
on the very first night

when there was no wrong
nor right

only a world apart

and the reckless pounding
of my heart

THIS LITTLE PIGGY

This little piggy played the violin,
this little piggy played drums,
this little piggy played sticks and bells,
this little piggy played none.

The last little piggy ran and ran all the way home,
hearing the lovely trio in his head,
but got so excited he wet himself . . .
which is where the WEE! WEE! WEE! comes from.

Soon thereafter, he taught himself to play piccolo
and stay dry.

IN MY DAY

When my father says, ". . . and *that's* how we did it in *my* day,"
I want to say, "So what? What good did it do you, your way

the real way the good way the only way?" I look at the way
my father stoops and I want to put my hands on his shoulders

and say, "There, Pops, stand up tall and fill your chest with air,"
but he mistakes my caring for criticism, and he hates to be

criticized. He thinks then I don't love him. But I do love him,
he who did it all so right, in his shining day, in his

shining way? I forgive him because, I suppose, his way is
the way of his mother, whom he remembers as perfect,

but who was in fact a tyrant. Yet, how can I forgive my father
but not his parents, who were surely as wretched

as their parents before them, caught as they all were in a web
of generational evil? I truly believe they all remember nothing

of that web. Instead, they remember the Christmas trees and
the upward tilted faces of their beloved children, whom they

adored, and who themselves will remember nothing until,
quite suddenly, they do, when they are half a century old.

FLYING NAKED OVER THE BLUE LAKE

And when I fly over the blue lake I haven't a stitch covering my body and I look down at the blue so far away, "Ahoy there!" I can feel the wind like feathers all over me on my stomach and my chest and on my legs and between my legs like a bird might feel in flight. I am warmth and bones and nerves and blood and muscle wrapped up in bare skin stretched tight, just skin between me and the wind like feathers touching from the outside that make me want more pleasure and more as I fly with my arms stretched out to the sides and my legs in a floating V, looking down over the endless blue lake.

GOLD LEAF

Ah! That's it!

All the men and boys
I made love to
were covered in gold leaf,

and off it fell
when I rolled over in bed,
one foot reaching for air.

AFRAID

When I was afraid,
I would count.

one thousand one
one thousand two

The plane will land.

one thousand three
one thousand four

The trunk will open.
The arm will move.
The scream will come.
The baby will be born.

one thousand fifty
one thousand fifty-one

Life is only seconds, they say,
one after the next and the next,
and on and on forever
until you die.

If that's really true,
why not fill
every second
with light?

one thousand one
one thousand two

Bright lights
shafts
rays
sparks

illuminating
the fear
until it blanches into
whiteness.

one thousand three
one thousand four

There is my hand,
on it my ring.
There is the window,
beyond it the blue sky.

There is my mother,
pouring a tea.
I am breathing,
in and out in and out.

One thousand five
One thousand six

I
am
not
afraid.

I am
Not

afraid

Not

afraid.

A SUDDEN DEER

A sudden deer,
a statue in the long grass,
shimmers in the biblical sunset
unexpectedly
interrupting
the careful patterns of
my elsewhere life.

GABE AT THREE

I brought you here
to this banquet of life
but neglected to give you
a plate, a fork, a knife—
the implements
you would need
in order to be . . .

But there you are at three, small body
top heavy
under immense headphones,
facing the picture window
and the wild roses.
The roses,

and all the earth's beauty
and all the earth's beauty
within you,
as you listen dreamily
to John Denver sing
Take me home, country roads . . .

BUCKET OF SNOW

Gabe Harris, age 3

"Mom, you know what I'm gonna do sometime? I'm gonna get a bucket and attach it to a string and fill the bucket with snow and hide there and then when someone comes along, I'll let go and the bucket'll drop on their head. Isn't that funny?"

LOGIC

Gabe Harris, age 3

Racing down the hall from Sunday morning "breffkis"
   with our orange juices, Gabe wins, as always.

"Do you know why I winned?"

"You poured it down your shirt when I wasn't looking?"

"It's because of that I know how to really slurp it!"

NARCISSUS BLADE

The fierce narcissus blade
cuts the midwinter snows
on its smooth strike
toward heaven.

SILVER BELLS

All unprotected was he.
But I did not see, I did not see.

When he was there in his room
I stood next to him, yet a thousand miles away.
I heard his small voice, but I did not listen.
Had I listened,
I would have heard
something as sweet as small silver bells.

But how could I have possibly listened
to his miniscule requests?
I was elsewhere, sorting out the buzz and whir
of voices in my own head.
Voices I did not yet know.
Voices I did not yet know.

Forgive me, my darling boy.

PHOBIA

I had learned how to endure it, how, in fact,
to bargain with it, to befriend it, to control it, to
accept it as a sickly inner shadow, and
with superhuman effort to bear it when it seemed
unbearable. We became partners, my phobia and I.

Then, after thirty-odd years of clumsily dancing with
my faithful partner,
I began
a process unlike any I had experienced up to that point.

I began deep-diving into the unconscious and discovering an
ever-growing community of inner beings; retrieving mem-
ories, drawing, painting, dancing, writing poetry, keeping a
journal; screaming, raging, smashing glass, finding the sor-
row beneath the rage, then soothing and comforting my now
intimate inner beings and myself; finding not only solace but
joy by bathing in the creek, having tea in our most floral cup,
watching an Attenborough series on monkeys, throwing
off my clothes and dancing under the full moon, no matter
where I was: in a pumpkin patch in Idaho, a fire escape in
Italy, a lakeside in Sardinia, or a copse in the Black Forest;
in short, transforming, finding freedom over mere function-
ality, healing rather than patching up, wholeness in place of
fractured shards.

There seemed to be no limits on what could unfold as I let
go of fear, little by little, eventually sending my dance part-
ner ingloriously into retirement—or on to do the foxtrot in
someone else's ballroom.

III.

FARMHOUSE

Four feet above the ground
in the blue dusk of winter,
past a field of whitewashed stones,
over a narrow country road

I glide in silence
past a farmhouse,
its windows undulating with yellow light
and movement within.

A dog lopes ominously,
a shadow along the hedge.
With a rumbling in his throat, he hastens
through the gate, wolf-rage building.

Then, furious and sudden, with a bubbling growl
he breaks upward through the frozen air,
white teeth strong and flashing:
snarling, raging, slashing.

In a smooth sidestep, I steer myself from reach
and float onward through my frozen journey—
unaffected by,
unconcerned with,

the chain-bound dog,
the cold,
the empty road,
the coming night.

ARTISTS' LIBERTY

There goes the infanta
  in a peasant dress
    dictating to the moon all
      the hollow mountain songs

of the cuckoo
  who sings from his burl these
    notes of gay divinity that echo
      high up in the Pyrenees.

The infanta translates:
  "Oh, dreamy orb, to thee I sing
    all of my finest offerings,
      pure and simple shall they ring."

The cuckoo has two silver notes
  with which to praise the light,
    the light from which the moon was made,
      and the infanta comes and goes,

      nature's tiny renegade,
       a whisper in a Spanish glade.

(In fact, the cuckoo is a nasty bird, who wears a slick, striped vest and who robs and steals, breaks into homes, kidnaps babies, then hides away in a wooden Swiss clock. Does his magical song forgive his cruel intent? It's an age-old unanswered question.)

LITTLE FELLOW

to a small dog and his mistress

Hey Little Fellow,
did we all take advantage of you
and your creeping age,
milky eyes
and cranky ways,
a difficult senior partner
enfeebled by passing years
and the mad rush of
changing times
places
people
things?

I wonder what it was like down there,
the long sharp grass
whistling over you
in the raging wind
that inhospitable day
you lay down flat
like a piece of earth
on the ground,
a silent wisp of dog
dreaming of warmth and stillness,
a kind word
a tidbit of
familiarity
an old routine
some peace.

Instead, well . . .
they almost killed you,
those idiots
they did not notice you napping
and ran flat over you!
Jesus, it was ghastly.
Your screams
reduced us all to helplessness
and contrition.
We'd have done anything
but there was almost nothing to do.
We could not prove anything
to you,
our size was useless
our greater wisdom
a myth.

But you stole past death and
you'll have some peace now
in the fresh cascades of remembered love
your mistress will bestow upon
your tiny mantle,
her tears a blessed rain from heaven
a windfall of life insurance
from the angels.

You see,
Little Fellow,
she was just distracted for a while,
people are like that
they forget
and block out
and are busy and away,

but in the moment of fire
she saw your valiant heart
and remembered you
and remembered you
and she clasped you to herself
like a severed limb to its origin
and fought for your life
by the minute as did you,
Little Fellow,
tough Little Fellow.
Ahhh,
here she is now.

There's nothing like a second chance,
Little Fellow,
is there?

GOD SONGS

The god songs
    cast upon the air
        from miniscule throats
            in feather veiled coats,

coax in the dawn
    hailing me ever on
        unfailingly.

May I respond this day
    to life and love
        as eloquently
            and as faithfully
                as they.

GRAY SEA

Oh, there's the sea:
capped and gray,
churning on forever
against the furious sky,
while a spray of tiny,
determined droplets
wings past my face.

A bead of water seized
by a tattered spiderweb
clings to the bouncing gossamer
and hangs all through the day
like silvery-white mercury.

When battle-gray evening comes,
the storm howls on.
The droplet sways tenaciously
through the sulphureous night,
and is still there when I rise
at dawn.

The coastal mist
lowers
lifts
gathers
shifts
sorts itself
and parts.

Heaven's flame will find me here
at the sacred mountains' edge.

Today, I am the shining tear
in the tattered spider's web.

FISHERMAN'S FINAL DREAM

on Katsushika Hokusai's Under the Wave off Kanagawa

Oh no, not this icy blue
rocking and weaving.

The fisherman's final dream is now,
slicing through the insistent sea with
death flakes falling all around.
Tiny stoics of grace,
frozen fingers on oars,
rowing toward their formal end
with no more power to direct their craft
than a maple leaf in a canyon waterfall.
Silent as the snow melting into their tunics,
the boats vanish into the looming whitecaps.
The snowflakes vanish.
The men vanish.

But they were never truly lost at sea,
for always on the distant horizon was
a famous snow-capped mountain—
as useful to them as an upside-down Dixie Cup.

A SCANT GRACE

on Grant Wood's American Gothic

Was it the icy, ruthless winters that caused them to
tuck in, to hoard? To shrink their lips into thin lines, to
practice frugality at every turn, to button up their senses?

They did not complain.

They rose at dawn—always—and knew work, hunger, thirst.
They lived their lives in Christ:
Cleanliness
Godliness
Severity
Sacrifice.

Death would be a welcome respite.

They said grace, but not *Amazing Grace*, only a scant grace
that spared sentiment and gratitude—it was resentment,
probably, for what must have felt like God's frugality to-
ward them.

ABSTINENCE

He was abstinent now but it was a constant battle to remain so
as his mother and father had been drinkers whose lives ended
early due to it, his father dying gray-lunged and inarticulate
in a hospital ward of men in agony who either coughed and
spat the life out of themselves or faded quietly into ghosts
in the early dawn as did he, and his mother two months lat-
er driving her big green Packard off a hairpin turn that fol-
lowed four warning signs—*Slow Down, Dangerous Curve
Ahead, Slippery When Wet, Trucks Use Low Gear*—on the
scenic route to the city, the one lined with Scotch broom and
poppies and bottlebrush and oak trees which she had taken
so seldom during all those years but, without knowing it, in
widowhood groped for something beautiful to present itself
to her as a reason to go on through the depressing business
of postmortem details, and somewhere she knew that she had
not really felt her husband since the drinking had settled in
on a grand scale many years ago, though she had loved him
very much in the early shining days of laughter and touch-
ing, and only after the second bit of news, the news about the
mother, had the son poured all the liquor in his house down
the toilet and thrown the bottles and the smell of them away
in paper sacks and sworn to all the angels in heaven he would
never touch a drop of alcohol again, and only later when the
vow became a reality did the sorrow of it all hit him with the
force of his father's hacking cough and speed of his mother's
plummeting Packard, and he saw with a terrible clarity that
the sorrow was generational and had killed them both and
was eating away at him, too, but he did not drink, he would
not could not drink, so he wept instead and cleansed himself
in salt water and does so still, and for all of that perhaps the
angels owe him some special kindness.

RAVENOUS

Quoth the raven:
"I am ravenous."
And he pecked out
Edgar Allan's eye.

COLLEEN

Colleen was timeless, I knew that immediately when I saw her for the first time in Pebble Beach, sitting in a rich lady's house wearing an orange shawl and orange lipstick, her smile so broad it was almost silly, her perfect teeth lined up like white corn kernels in a row and sky-blue eyes and blond hair that flowed onto and over her shoulders, her posture straight and strong as she sat there across from me in the room of a dying girl who was fading quickly and without grace, lying there between us as I tried to sing "Barbara Allen" to her, and Colleen encouraged me with that smile and those eyes.

Those were the days when Lucas was still sitting beside Colleen, the beloved handsome Lucas who was like springtime in her life, who loved her children, who was full of life and laughter until one day he slid and slipped in his little car in the fog and the mist of Monterey pines on the slick sea-wet road, and Colleen tried to pull his life back into his body as all around her in the chaos people were lying and telling her he'd be alright, he'd be fine, but his soul was floating up all bewildered into the fog and the mist, and it kept going until it was beyond the fog and beyond the mist and beyond reach in a kind of hazy limbo where decisions are made by someone else, and then his ghost came down and hovered over the wreck on the sea-wet road and saw what had happened, but it was not perturbed because it had already seen the light, had already begun dancing in the light, that same light hospital patients sometimes see as death approaches on glorious wings.

And in the days and weeks that followed, the ghost sifted through the walls and sat up near the ceiling and attended the nightmare he had left behind on earth, and she understood that he was around, so she went silently out into the patio in her silk turquoise robe and there she sat and waited for him to pass by like a riffle of warm wind and he did and he whispered in her ear, *It's only a matter of time, Co.*

She had an exceptional sense of cosmic proportion, which suggested to her that a human being in the larger scheme of things is about the size of an ant, and that your time on this particular planet is only a blink, and that when you leave you probably just float around in the universe until the people you really belong to come and join you, so Colleen filled in her time in a distant-present sort of way, in a splendid manner mind you with her flowing hair and dancing eyes and dazzling smile that knocked men off their feet and right into the hedge where they didn't even feel the prickles in their asses because they were looking at her, a kind of absent-minded goddess of rainbows, as she went about raising her children and traveling around the world and living on a windy pier over a merry-go-round with its calliope wheezing away from nine a.m. till midnight in the summers, and giving away everything she owned and getting involved and getting arrested and adoring her kids but very few others because the adoring spot in her heart had already been spoken for.

So while Lucas floated around the universe checking in occasionally, Colleen floated around on earth checking out as often as possible, and on her seventieth birthday she was more beautiful than she was at forty, surrounded by friends and family and ex-lovers and she was shining and laughing and happy and grateful for the warmth and love, and when she went to bed that night she whispered to Lucas that all these wonderful people showed up for her birthday party and he whispered back, *That's because they love you, Co* and he asked, *How's earth? What time is it? Let me check your watch . . . my, how time flies! You'll love it up here . . . the air's clean as a whistle! I miss you. I love you. It's only a matter of time, Co.*

THE ROSY TRUMPETEERS

by Yasha

She could not take
the swift and certain knife
and strike nor hovering death
nor lingering life.

Her body ached
from holding up that sword,
as though attending
some unspoken word,
till brittle boned and frail, she
folded in upon herself,
all senses gone,

cloistered in a darkened room
of musky sheets
and final fever gown.

As if suspended, we surrounded her
and, leaning in and arching
like protective boughs,

we ministered to her breathing,
counting long and longer
pauses in between
each rasping breath

until, at last,
the Rosy Trumpeteers arrived
and pried the saber
from her eagle grip.

They held it upward for a silver second,
turned it back, and cut her
swiftly, softly
through her velvet heart.

That barely beating
yet unbeaten heart
had soldiered her unquestioningly
through fifty-seven years.

Oh, *she* had questioned, yes,
and often,
perched atop the ocean cliffs
as silent and as steadfast as a
pre-storm gull in flight pondered
meter, inch, and impact,
pondered childhood lost
and demons
and eternal night.

Long before the illness
she had spoken of her
darkening reveries.

"The thing that keeps returning
to my mind," she said,
"is: *Do I leave it here,
or do I take my purse with me?*"

Hers was not an ordinary face.
It was a visage deftly
carved in smoky marble,

loomed in tapestry
and brilliant shards of art—
a face of Aztec ancestry.

Yet, she had known
it was not a useful thing
that men would fall into her eyes
and drown
in blue and green
of lake and moss,
white of a conjured wedding gown.

And now within the shimmering grasses
of the cliffs, she saw reflected all of this
and more.

Alas.

For she was not to hear
the Rosy Trumpeteers
high-stepping past.

No, she would not have seen
the ribboned tambourine
the dancing pipers
and the painted drum
until the latening hours
and the dreadful
sinking of the sun,
until the final turning
of the hourglass,
the stilling of the pendulum.

Then and only then
could her heart end its tireless task.

Then and only then,
as illness vanquished every
peerless ray of sun
still glistening
on the landscape of her past,

the heart,
like every muscle in her ravaged body,
yearned to rest
and gladly did it yield
to the final cut.

Her spirit lingered for a restless second
then sped upward and away,

leaving behind for those of us
left standing at the precipice of time
a score of vivid painted images
upon the pages of our lives,
upon the pages of our lives.

As the Rosy Trumpeteers proclaimed
the end of one small life,

her form rose gladly,
her spirit newly peaceful
looked to Earth
and wondered,
as it faded into darkness,
on the whereabouts of its rebirth.

THE PLANET EASTER

The Easter egg is a lonely planet.
It is covered with decal bunnies
and children's art
and sits alongside
sugar-flecked candy chickies
and silver kisses
on tissue paper grass
in a basket half hidden
behind a clump of daffodils.

The sun is a huge weightless egg of pure white
with an oval picture window on one side
framed by a sugary braid of pastels
and inside is
a miniature rabbit family
with long ears and cotton tails,
parasols and hoop skirts;
the daddy is wearing a tuxedo
and they are picnicking in the grass.

This is not a time to feel
evil in the air,
evil slipping into me
slipping into me.
No, I'm not going to
sunrise service to see
the cross silhouetted against yellow dawn;
there might be somebody up there
this time.

Somewhere in the shy cavity that was my mother then
on the Easter morn of 1947,
somewhere under the cover of her new polka-dot dress
and lavender perfume and broad-brimmed hat and white gloves,
her heart must have been
twisted at the throat
to keep from screaming out
"Oh, my babies
Oh, my darling babies!"

Had she only known,
she surely would have rushed into the evil
with a flaming ax.
Had she only been aware
and hacked it to bits,
and then reached for her three babies
with strong arms open,
and we would have come tumbling
across the twirling dark heavens,
naked and sore in our fresh dresses.

We knew all along
and in spite of everything
that our proper place
was in the arms of our pretty mother.

Rocking us on the sandbox ledge,
high heels off and
bare feet planted
in the grass that grows to the edge
of the pansy bed,
she will yet sing to us in a whisper:
"On the mountain stands a lady.
Who she is I do not know . . .

All she wants is gold and silver.
All she wants is a nice young man . . ."
while counting out jelly beans
and dropping them into our Easter baskets.

YOSEMITE

A brace of people
loiters around
the bus stop
in the chilly parking lot
at the mountain lodge.

Who could they be
with their scraggly hair
and tattoos
wrist collars
logo'd leathers
and rumpled shirts untucked over
stiff jeans that shine with burnished dirt?

Who are these furtive-eyed masters of darkness,
these infant Satans
ignoble nomads
whose fat women and slat-sided girls
hide somewhere within their own flesh
and attach themselves
by short leashes of their own making
to the dog-men?

Who are these empty ladies,
with their dark agendas
ignited by the danger
of the netherworld,
these crusty maidens
with extinct childhoods
who buy up loyalty at the flea market,

then give it for free to
their masters?

I think they were once infants
whose souls were stolen away in the night
as they lay in their white cribs
gazing milk-mouthed and wordless
at the leafy designs
on their nursery's whispering curtains.
They've come to see the deafening waterfalls,
and the reflection of
the empyrean mountain peaks
shimmering orange and gold
in the little pools of dawn
that gather on the river's shores.

They've come to the high mountains
in search of their lost soul parts,
which have long since learned
to run with the stag
nest with the eagle
sing with the crickets
and dance with the wolves.

WHITECAPS

All my babies died
   and became tiny whitecaps
      on a softly rolling sea.

And while elsewhere,
   in some nether land
      the cruel and raging winds
         lashed at my tethered heart,

   my babies
      bobbled
         like tub toys
            and slept on.

LAUGHTER AND COGNAC, 1944

to Ginetta

I will not forget you.

You, with the crusade banners
in your crowded heart
wild birds in your hair
WWII on your white forehead
a matchbox in your frozen hand.

A NARROW ESCAPE

Which will snap first?
The rope,
pulling pulling
the branch,
bending bending
the neck,
stretching stretching
the life
hanging by
a thread?

Or did they mean to say
by a rope?
So narrow the old rope
all shredded and moldy,

so heavy the man
struggling, kicking.
Will it be a tie?
No, the rope is already tied

to the man.
The man has
not quite died . . .
SNAP
goes the rope,
PLOP
goes the man.
A narrow escape!

WRITING

Writing is like love,
it can't be forced
or it dies in its own process.

Writing is like love,
it can't be forced
or it becomes
cement
in a tube of toothpaste.

STAR: A REVERY

by Star

By the time I was seven
I had a wild heart.
They called me Star.

From paper cutouts
I fashioned an elegant bandit
and shadowed his face
on my pillow
by the soft and leafy light
of the streetlamp.

I gave my outlaw a wild heart
to match my own
and a black horse
to run side by side with my white mare
in the runaway circus.

In the Sears and Roebuck catalog
was a photograph of
white drum majorette boots
with tassels.

In my violet rhapsodies I had those boots
and pure blond hair
and the blue satin flair skirt and matching cape
that my mother made.

I would twirl right out the screen door
and across the wooden porch

down to the lawn
with gopher lumps of damp sod
and fallen leaves
and past the autumn ripe apple trees
to the circus of flags
(the pigpen next door
where lives a grand old pig
with her piglets)
and I'd twirl my sequined baton
with agility
and fling it high up into the air
and follow its spangled course with an easy eye
and catch it clean and simple
when it came down.

And I'd shake my pure blond curls
away from my eyes
and break a pretty sweat
and balance the spinning baton
on my fingertips
like an offering
and a challenge
to be outdone.

And my majorette boots will never miss a beat
of the award-winning clown musicians playing
"Be Kind to Your Web-Footed Friends"
and I'm smiling sixty to the dozen
the whole time
while executing the perfect performance
the prize-winning performance
and the big sow next door nudges her piglets
and they all stand up and wait for the tune to end

and then they cheer
and stomp in the mud
and say I am the greatest baton twirler
Clarence Center has ever known!

And that's how I got my name:

Star.

HERON AND BLACKBERRIES

A great blue heron
glides the width of the creek
over a distant pool,
which is covered in chartreuse moss.

He sweeps down through the oaks
and admires his reflection
in the ripples.

Down the creek,
my mother is lost in her
endless fight for more blackberries,
her staff propped against
stone, mugwort, and fallen leaves.

She does not see
the heron's effortless flight
as it falls upward
into the sky.

BIG SUR

for Gabe at 24

Here is a cruel beauty.
Here is thunder and flying mist,
craggy granite beds
of tiny wildflowers
and mother of pearl tears
glistening down the fierce cheeks
of red clay ghosts.
Here is the sound of wind
like a forsaken witch
sobbing along the crow fly cliffs,
lost in the nether sky,
defeated by the coast's brutal beauty.

A pure white heron,
the king of Castle Rock,
preens above silhouettes
of hunching brown herons
lined up like nuns along the rocks
and down to the raging sea.

I thought I saw the reef of jade
dancing in a renegade
shaft of sunlight, too,
and chunks of broken rocks
strewn like emeralds
all along the sand.

And then I saw my son,
my only son, my red clay son,

my soulmate son,
as he was crouched birdlike
high atop a massive rock,
high above the deafening sea.
And as I watched him prayerfully,
he spread his arms,
reached for the shaft of sunlight,
then looked down and smiled at me
the smile of a thousand suns.

Sun of heavens,
pierce the sky
and shine upon
my only boy,
who radiates
like you, today.

My son's a thousand sons in one.
And I am neither witch, nor nun,
nor heron white, nor blue nor brown,
I am the Mom, the only one:
the mother of my only son.

PERFECT

It wasn't until Pelican was dying
that he discovered perfection.

He had moments of the purest joy.
He saw mountains unveiled.
His heart burst from his body and danced.
He threw his stodgy notions to the wind
and felt the rain on his head
and the crumbling earth beneath his sneakers.

That final spring in the Alps,
all the academic nonsense
all the soulless questions
begging debatable answers,
simply evaporated for moments at a time
leaving him quizzically lightheaded and airy,

as though he could have lifted off
from the porch of the ristorante
like a condor. He could have
floated around aimlessly
counting clumps of wildflowers
that clung to the bright rocks
and nestled in the grassy crevasses
of the high mountains.

The scholarly questions
were merely weird translations of
"Where's my mother?
I'm so sleepy."

which echoed forth
from his early childhood
as he waited for her
at the top of the stairs,

his little frame
invisible to the household
as he murmured,
"Are you coming soon?"

Pelican lay dying in his familiar bed
of shared friendship and imperfect matrimony.

In this moment,
fear had escaped him;
tiredness was pleasant,
and there was no pain.

He was holding his cup of tea
and pointing out the sunlight on the garden.
"Look at the roses!" he said. "I've never
seen roses like that! They're perfect!"

Pelican forgot his name,
or rather, who he was. "Am I Robin?"
(His eldest son, who sat next to him.)
"Or am I Pelican?"

"You are Pelican."

"Ah yes!" said Pelican. "What was I saying?"

"About Italy . . ."

"Ah yes! I loved Italy,"
he beamed.
"Loved it!
Yes!"

He punched the air with his fists,
delightedly.
"It was perfect!"
And then he rested.

His wife approached,
framed by the brightness
of their bedroom window,
and carrying a cognac.

Pelican steadied his teacup
as he reached toward her silhouette,
"Mother! There you are! I knew you'd come!"
He smiled radiantly and said: "Perfect!"

JIMI

You performed just before me
at the Isle of Wight
and somehow
lit
the
stage
on fire.

I performed
in your wake
as the aftermath
flickered down through
the floodlights.

I sang

"Strike another match go start anew!"
and "Look out the saints are coming through!"

You were no saint
but you certainly came through.

You
came
through
like a
magnificent
natural
disaster

like a fucking volcano.

At Woodstock
you eviscerated the national anthem
and made it your own.
There were no bombs bursting in air
and rockets red glare.

There was only your guitar
and 400,000 souls electrified
in the dawn's early light

out there in the mud

out there in the volcanic ash.

And you were only twenty-seven when you died.

JUDY

Backstage,
we embraced.

I buried my face in my hands

and the conversation
we've never had tumbled out.

"It was a long road,"
you said.

"Forgive me for never being there,"
I said.

I buried my face in my hands;
you buried your son in the ground.

PORTRAIT

After e. e. cummings

Robert Zimmerman
blue-eyed son from Duluth
    used to
        scribble thought-dreams
onetwothreefourfive songs justlikethat
      brilliant stuff
he was a brilliant kid.
      And what I want to know is
who's writing that kind of stuff today,
Mister Creator?

DEAR LEONARD

by Joan and Yasha

Dear Leonard,

I remember 1960-something, that filthy hotel restaurant in the Village, some man throwing up in the phone booth off the lobby, and you, Leonard, my unlikely dinner host. *Seconal & Razor Blades*, we called you. King of black predictions. Harbinger of a scorched earth.

Yet, from your canopied dreams did the sisters of mercy drift up, lovely and winking, full of folly. And Suzanne, that careless ghost, pure as our young beliefs, beautiful as the new age, daughter of the dawn of Aquarius, an absent-minded seductress hurling tote bags of goodness to the dreamers stuck in line at Woodstock. And Joan of Arc and Bernadette and all the other little birds on wires. So much beauty from so much darkness. *What a gift.*

But now I'm thinking of 1993, Leonard, when I listened to your wordless song "Tacoma Trailer" while I sat on a hotel room windowsill in Würzburg, Germany, and watched a snowstorm tear past in horizontal white splendor. As your piano chords filled my chest, I saw, plain as life itself, a tattered little boy appear outside, straining uphill against the storm. He wore tattered shorts, a too small jacket, and ruined shoes. I brought him up with my eyes into the warmth of my room and into the shelter of my arms.

From your canopied dreams came this boy who spoke his own lyrics to your melody:

Take these silver pools from my eyes, I am ever so young, and my knees are blue from the cold and my hands are frozen.

My name is Yasha. I am twelve years old. My family was all killed in a holocaust—my mother I don't remember except that she was dark and beautiful; my father, nothing; my sisters and brothers, nothing.

Do you suppose he doesn't know the war is over? Do you think, Leonard, that I am one of your sisters of mercy? Or just a vessel in which to hold this miraculous boy?

Yasha turned to leave, but I pled with him to stay. He told me:

I shall go back out into the driving snow and the little silver pools in my eyes will freeze over and I will be blind with no more reason to go on, and I can lie down in the snow then, and I will hear music of violins and rich cellos, and I will die. This is the simplest and it is what I expect.

"Oh no," I whispered. "Stay with me! It would break my heart if you left me here when I've only just found you!"

What do you make of it, Leonard? Your past life or mine? Hitler became "chancellor" in 1933. You were born in 1934. I was all of four years old when the Third Reich came to its murderous end in 1945. Are we only us, Leonard, or are we many at once?

Yasha reached for the cup of hot coffee, and I saw his hands were delicate and white. He said, softly:

When I close my eyes, I see old cities deserted, fallen birds in the snow, and a white horse on the icy road pulling a cart of vegetables . . . but I see bones sticking out, white as the snow that vanishes upon them.

Was there no love at all in the world when I came into it? Was it run only by blue-eyed sons of Satan in their tall proud boots of glistening leather which mirrored back the common faces bloated with pain and gaunt with hunger and here and there a clump of hair mixed with mud and dirt?

But this is what they told me was beautiful back then . . . everything all backwards . . . I am brought up all backwards.

Take these silver pools from my eyes. For you they will become summer lakes, dreamlike under linden trees, blue and clear and full of shining fish.

Evening came and, exhausted, Yasha slept. Deep in the night, he stirred and, half awake, said quietly:

Joan thinks I should stay on this earth . . . she thinks I am a kind of genius and could create beauty in an uncommon way . . . for the moment there is calm . . . I can see clumps of snow on pine boughs outside . . . I hear music, music coming from the air around me . . . the song is so familiar . . .

Yasha remained for a time, writing unique and exquisite poems. I can't wait for you to hear them, Leonard! He honors you, making so much beauty from so much darkness.

SILENCE

In the noisiest era since time began
there are yet ways to be still and quiet—
to say a hushed grace before the evening meal,
to walk the streets of a city and meet only with our eyes
the eyes of the reflective and the lonely.
We must bring our silence with us.

The only intersection in my town, once scarcely used,
now thrums with people and cars.
Soon there will be a streetlight.
One of the dwindling families of deer that inhabits
the vanishing hills braved that intersection the other day, and
we became quiet as they stepped gingerly across our hearts.
They brought their silence with them.

In the hum of the meadow opposite my house, I picked
yellow tarweed and placed it on the mantle in a blue vase.
It smelled like the damp wildness of all seasons.
From within the unruly bouquet a cricket's song rang out,
a noisy announcement of such cheer that it stopped me still.
I breathed it into the bottom of my feet.

But the sound that resounded in my ears was
the echoing stillness that followed.
I stood by the mantle and waited and waited.
I held my breath.
He brought his silence with him.

BIRDSONG

I lay out on the porch in the dark
in my warm and rumpled sheets

awakened by the moon-sliver
casting glimmers on the hibiscus.

It is time for the most beautiful music to begin.
Heart awaiting, every nerve listening.

But by dawn's light, we heard it not
and my breath grew silent, but we heard it not.

I was perched in a nightdress
at the edge of the veranda in anticipation.

But we heard it not. Yes, today was
the day the birdsong suddenly stops.

Last year it was on the fifteenth of June,
so I'd hoped I had more time.

But when I could distinctly make out
tree against tree on the mountain across the canyon,

I knew it was true: there was no flood, no chorus.
Only cheeps and peeps, chirps, squawks, and eeps.

But the ringing of hundreds of silver throats would not
come again until spring—if they ever come at all.

I told myself, "It is nature . . . the birds
have business . . . or are tired." I held my breath.

I can barely stand the inevitable turning
of the seasons and the remnants and shadows

of the hosannas that filled the canyon
only yesterday.

ON THE OTHER HAND

How very silly
of me
to leave my purse
full of grown-up stuff
unattended
around my granddaughter
when she is only three.

I should have brought her

a miniature music box,
a tea set with
cups the size of acorn caps,
a beaded necklace
of many colors,
a squeeze and glow flashlight,
or maybe
an automatic bubble-blower,
giant Legos,
even a—god forbid—Barbie doll.

On the other hand,

she had a blast
digging into my purse,
scooping out curls of rosy blush
with her fingernails,
sucking on the powder brush,
painting an armchair
with lip gloss,

sprinkling the dog
with *eau de cologne*.

Soon, my granddaughter was

pocketing dimes and quarters,
tossing bills into the air
and giggling to herself,
then hiding in the closet
with her grandmother's
driver's license
to chew on
and a fistful of
credit cards
to hide
in her dad's
dirty socks.

JASMINE

Ahhhhhhhh,
the sweet scent of
milk bubbles
from your
perfect
tiny
lips.

You belch,
and the universe applauds.

LOW-LOW IMPACT CLASS

At the 6:00 a.m. low-low impact class in my local gym
the crepe-skinned ladies
with nets over their pin curls,

small humps on their backs,
soft webs at the elbow bend,
and no bottoms to speak of,

do the power walk,
knee bends, and surprisingly confident
leg lifts to the pulsing beat of

"I Will Survive," music thoughtfully chosen by
the smiling twenty-three-year-old instructor whose skin is
tight and lustrous and whose head is full of dry leaves,

who chides *Come on, ladies! Come on, ladies!*
The old girls push on,
stay the course, and last a full hour.

Afterwards, they have a lovely steam bath
and a shower, dry off, powder their parts, then
maneuver their bodies into street clothes.

They take out pin curls and comb up,
apply cheeks, lips, and eyes,
pack wet towels into fluorescent gym bags,

and with endorphin counts that would
put their middle-aged kids to shame,
head rosily out to greet the rising winter sun.

THELMA

My hens make a soft clacking sound
when they snatch a leaf of
Swiss chard from my hand,
click
clack
like old man geezer teeth
and sprint off,
their yellow, corrugated legs
flying straight out
to the right
and to the left
hurdling the ground cover,
squawking uphill
to the geraniums.

Happy rivulets from the green garden hose
spread down to meet them,
and they go a-huntin'
in the wet earth for
bugs
and spiders
gnats
and mosquitoes,
in the oak leaves
and mottles of sun
on the brown earth
that's brown like Thelma,

who scuttles off to dry dirt,
clickety clack

scritch scratch.
Thelma claws the earth,
scratches and flings
making large flecky dust clouds
and shaping herself a tub
of dry heat
and remnants of summer.

Thelma rolls around,
flattening her fluffy bosom
into the dusty little crater,
stretches her legs
flaps onto her side
puffs over to the other side
furiously pecks a little white underfeather from the air
and finally settles down,
flattening again
so she's kind of spread out and listing,
peering over the walls of her stronghold
toward the vegetable garden.

Thelma, bless your tiny heart.

How about some carrot greens and sweet potato?

Here, I'll mince it up for you,
and in exchange you'll give me a
brand
new
egg!

I didn't realize Thelma's egg would be wet when it
plopped out into the new world.

Of course it was!
Just like a baby elephant, a newborn sparrow,

Or me.
Or you.

VIVIAN

I wish said Viv I'd been able to talk to my mother while she was still alive and healthy but I was so pissed off back then I just stayed away thank you very much and never went by or phoned until she was sick with cancer and even then she was unbearable controlling my brother and me from her wheelchair—the minute you disagreed with her on anything she'd lean forward like *this* with her eyes shut and rock back and forth with her hands around her knees where the pain was or even worse she'd interrupt you and say would you be a darling and get my codeine pills from the medicine cabinet

I was married and living over here when they called to say she was dying oh God and I didn't want to go in fact I got hysterical I was so scared of being in the room with a dying person poor Terry he drove me to Santa Cruz you know over those beautiful winding hills and I didn't even see them because I was screaming and crying and I'm surprised Terry didn't throw me off a cliff but when we got to the hospital I splashed cold water on my face and smoothed my hair and found her room and stuck my head in and get this it was serene and calm and so was mom

I took her hand and suddenly wasn't the least bit afraid anymore isn't that amazing she had this little blue blanket over her and I pulled it up to cover her chest and sat down and read her Emily Dickinson and she stopped me at one point and told me in this raspy voice that she had done the best she knew how to and even if she'd made some mistakes she had in fact loved us and I said I love you too mom and you know I think I did right then

I had my hand on her heart when it stopped beating but just before it did she said I hear my mother calling me my mother is calling me and I asked what is she saying and she answered in a singsong voice the way you call a child home from down the block at the end of the day *Lor-ray-ain Lor-ray-ainnn* and again real slow *Lor-raaaay-ainnn* which was her mother's name and then she was gone

THE CAPTAIN NAPS

The lines are out.
The captain naps.
The surface swells.
The waves cap.

The winds change.
The sails flap.
The fish bites.
The lines snap.

Elsewhere . . .

the sloppy kisses
of the koi
break the stillness
of the rich man's pond.

FIVE ANGELS

White trees in a field of ash
beneath the moon's pale arc.

Five angels creep up
from their graves.
One carries a little basket of stars
and a gold manicure set
in a forest green leather case
which they open,
chatter over softly,
then sit themselves down
on a slick marble slab
and messily paint each other's nails
a garish red.
They are somber
and very very beautiful
there on the white marble
in the white ashes
in the shadows of the white trees
under the protective arc
of the weeping moon

who knew them, you see,
before.

DOG DEATH HEAT

There is a dog death heat
on the rippling desert.

There is a tambourine
song shout procession,

and a child sweat face
of darkness.

Somewhere
over the dunes
there is
water,

I promise.

IV.

NOWADAYS

my father in his 93rd year

Nowadays
his thoughts
and words
escape on wings
into
the elegant
draping vines
of the weeping willow

and time is lost.

But he is found
and blind no more to me.

Long after his death,
I saw my father
at the hotel pool,
young, brown, and guileless
sucking in his tummy,
jumping in.

He started the sidestroke.

Swim, Pops, I said silently.
And silently he said,
Oh, how I've missed this.

And he swam and swam,
back and forth

end to end
beginning to end
all health and happiness.

This was my father,
young and happy.

This was me,
overflowing with love.

PEACHY

Mom lived to be one hundred.

She told us she'd stay around
as long as we kept her entertained.
Eventually, Mom grew bored
with our entertainment
and retired from the public life

she'd enjoyed in her
one-room cottage:
receiving guests, offering tea,
chatting to visitors.
Mom took to her bed.

In her late nineties,
she peers up at us from
her thick pillow in
its freshly ironed pillowcase
as we busy ourselves with her care.

Our names are gone,
but our faces
glide pleasantly around the bright
room and bring her a kind of
safety and comfort.

She doesn't mind anymore
that someone must clean up her messes.
"Oh, phew, it stinks!" she says.
"Never mind," we say.
"In a minute you'll smell peachy."

And she does, with pink cheeks
and apricot shift
and copper earrings,
gold flecked eyes
and a dab of vintage perfume.

Mom floats away into a memory
of when she was three:
She is dressed in a white pinafore
covered with violet and purple
mulberry stains,

staring dreamlike at the brook
that gurgles quietly,
hypnotically.
She inches toward
the water.

She balances on the
soft pebbles
and splashes her
little feet
in the ripples.

And now, smiling up from her pillow,
she wipes her hands
on her pinafore
and holds up an offering
of invisible mulberries to us.

"Do you want one?" she asks,
motioning as though popping

a few dark berries into
her open mouth
and making chewing motions.

"Love one!" we say in unison,
and take the invisible berries from
her outstretched hand and chew them
and swallow them
and say, "Mmmmm! Yum!"

Mom smiles slyly
and thinks to herself,
"Ha-ha, smarty pants.
Those are not real berries.
Those are pretend berries!"

She continues to chew,
and in the sweet-smelling room, each of us
feels quite peachy.

QUEEN OF THE MOUNTAIN

by B. B. and others

Pauline was the shadow sister out in the dusty hills
   who made wildflowers pop up from the ground
      in full flower just by singing softly
         over the meadow grass,
           she was the quiet one.

She was a beauty.
   Thick brown hair and honey skin
      in the sun, she'd turn gold and copper,
         her hazel eyes were huge
           and her hands were able.

Pauline was so shy she could become invisible.
   She moved away from the loud busy world,
      became a mistress of the "Silent Arts"
         and sewed beauty into fabrics
           the way a spider weaves silk into her web.

And that way she didn't have to be sad anymore.

She once made us a quilted robe of
   red velvet so dark it was smoky,
      which she got at a vintage booth
         in the flea market
           for very little money, I'm sure.

Then there was the silver and purple brocade cloth
   from the bazaar in Istanbul,
      and the great black silk scarf from Spain

with giant roses embroidered on, bright red
with green leaves and curlicues and tassels.

It was an inside-outside robe,
so we could wear it either way
depending on the mood or the weather.
She filled the pockets with homemade
bundles of lavender from her garden.

Pauline was famous far and wide in those hills
for the mud house she built
into the mountain,
all by hand
and all by herself.

Only she,
the Queen of the Mountain,
could build a castle
out of nothing but what surrounded her:
straw and water and dirt,

branches, stones,
junk, metal, glass,
broken pottery, bits of statues,
and planks left over
from half-built cabins.

The only rule was the material had to be used
just how you found it—you couldn't cut it or chop it,
it just had to fit in—the way she didn't
when they tried her whole lifetime
to shape her into the wrong patterns.

The mud house had three floors,
  which you reached by climbing the inside stairs
    of giant tree roots,
      some places too dark to see,
        some too small to squeeze through.

On the sunny side the windows were made of
  thick blue bottles and thick red bottles
    (all with bits of dirt inside that never came out),
      so the light cast into the murky rooms
        on dust flecked sunbeams was purple.

Cubbyholes carved into the rock-hard walls
  held mystical things, spooky things:
    a mask, a moleskin medicine bag, a squirrel skull,
      a deer foot, carved wooden frames with
        ancient photographs of our ancestors

when they were young
  in their white starched collars,
    brooches and britches,
      eyes staring out furtively
        and forlornly.

The main house was spooky, too.
  It was dark inside,
    hand hewn scratchy wood hidden behind velvet curtains,
      and a film of valley dust
        coating everything.

The entire house was small enough to be
  heated with one
    steel and iron

stand-alone wood stove
Joan gave her back in the '60s.

There was an outhouse
fifty feet away from the main house and
to get there, you had to walk a narrow dirt pathway.
But she and her husband,
who was just as much of a hermit as she was,

planted poppies and snapdragons for beauty,
and sage and jasmine for the heavenly odor
(which was stronger than the outhouse smell),
so when you sat there, the wind whooshed
the good smell up and over the stinky part.

One day we had great cause for celebration
because Pauline got a washing machine,
and a wringer like
the one Joan's mom had in the cellar in 1945,
just after washboards.

Pauline made other houses, too.
One in an old Volkswagen bus shell
with vines all around.
One on a mountaintop,
built of adobe bricks we helped make.

I mean, we actually made the bricks from scratch.

And one in a circle of madrone trees
where she pushed heaps of brush and weeds
into a bigger circle ten feet away from the construction,

so the rats would settle there instead of
   in her new home, which of course they did.

Once, we caught her
   hunched over a roadside rock
      whispering to a baby rattlesnake
         "You go hide," she was saying.
            "It's not safe here."

And he did her bidding.

And then there were the black widow spiders
   on the top floor of the mud house,
      which she scolded back into their darkened corners
         because their shiny bodies and red hourglass markings
         would frighten a normal person.

One morning, she was on her daily walk
   up the canyon
      on the winding path,
         humming,
            the smell of damp earth all around her,

wearing one of the robes she'd made from
   that dark velvet
      and maybe a crown of gold
         melted by the sun
            to fit her noble head to perfection.

And then, right there on the path
   twenty feet in front of her
      was a mountain lion,
         staring her in the face
            his yellow cat's eyes like shiny marbles.

"Were you scared?" we asked, huddling around her.
  "Oh no," she said, "I just told him 'Hello Beast,
    this is my path and we can share it.
      But right now, I'm on my walk
        and I need the right of way.'"

And the mountain lion loped away through the dead leaves,
miner's lettuce, and thistles.

One night Pauline and a friend from the outside
  were looking up at the starry night sky and
    the new guy said:
      "That's Orion! And there's his belt
        and over in back of us is the big dipper

(big arm swoop), which makes THAT the North Star!"
  And Pauline said,
    as if peering lazily down
      from another galaxy,
        "Who cares?"

Then one day she got really sick and was taken
  to the hospital, muttering, "What a nuisance."
    And, to the nurses tiptoeing around her bed
      pointing out what those gray marks on
        her lung meant,

she said, "Who cares?"

After a time,
  she gathered all the family around, and said,
    "Seventy-seven? That's enough. I've decided to check out."

And she quit eating.
 Then she quit drinking.

We were there in the hospital with her
 for as long as it took.
  I, B. B., was a wreck, crying all the time because
  all Pauline wanted was a cookie
   but her kids and husband

thought it would be unhealthy
 and made gritty-looking green drinks instead,
  which she drank dutifully
   because she'd never learned how to say
    No to anybody, especially her family.

So I'd smuggle in cookies and Snickers bars
 and also sneak extra drips of morphine into the tube
  whenever the coast was clear,
   because she hurt.
    And she'd make a little smile in her sleep.

Joan sat on the hospital bed and cried and cried,
 and told Pauline how much she loved her,
  and how lucky she was to be her sister,
   and all of a sudden Pauline up and said,
    "Mmm, I guess this calls for a hug . . ."

Then we all cried because she'd never said anything like that
before.

And the doctors knew and we knew and she knew
 what was coming. It was staring her in the face
  like the mountain lion with the shiny yellow cat's eyes

and she didn't seem to be any more scared of death than
she was of meeting a mountain lion on her canyon walk.

Or if she was scared, she didn't say so.
She probably wouldn't want to be a nuisance,
or maybe it was all the same to her
when she whispered softly,
"Hello Beast,

this is my path.
Right now, I'm on my walk
and I need the right of way . . ."
and she turned on her side and closed her eyes
and the room went very quiet indeed.

And now, Pauline belongs to the mountain
and the mountain belongs to her.
The lion waits on the pathway.
And the little snake licks the air.
The black widow spiders on the third floor

scuttle and wonder where

she might be,

the shadow sister

with the auburn hair,

their Queen of the Mountain.

JUST BECAUSE

Just because you were ill
and frail
and ice-filled
and hated us all,
didn't mean we would
give up on you, little sister.

When you'd had enough of Western meds,
the hypodermics of poison,
the MRIs,
the brain fog,
the morphine patches,
and the pretending,

we tried
potions and crystals,
tumor whisperers,
praying nuns,
homeopathic granules,
and telepathic white light.

And then: Switzerland!
We'd heard of miraculous cures from there.
On the way to the airport, I tried to
give you my most precious prayer beads,
but you turned to the window and said,
"I already have some."

Maybe in Switzerland they would
fill your veins with gold

and flood your tumors with light,
and return you to us whole
and full of forgiveness.

And I?
I saw that when I inched closer
to your well-guarded boundaries,
my very presence
was unbearable to you.

We were bonded to one another in
Love,
but the complexities of our lives
had left us at each other's mercy
and no place around
was there safety to be found.

Switzerland sparked hope in you,
and the forces in your life
that kept you mummified
went briefly idle.

In your absence, I went off
to meditate on a cold hillside
with Buddhists,
wild turkeys,
mad crows,
and the full moon.

While you were in Switzerland,
you could breathe on your own
in your small, immaculate room.
But the miracle we'd prayed for
didn't come and you were left exhausted.

Back home, in the airport,
you turned to us, raised your arm in the air,
feigning an opera diva,
and attempted a triumphant high note.
But your voice, weakened by illness,
had lost its strength and beauty.

The high note
stopped prematurely,
ending in a little cough that
became ragged and spasmodic
and didn't bring anything up,
but stayed dry as dust.

Mimi, my beautiful little sister,
you danced with death
until you were spent.
Its long shadow finally enveloped you
and stole you away from those you loved
and those you hated.

But surely,
just because we were clumsy
and desperate
and in your way,
didn't mean
you would give up on us.

TREMORS

I lost my balance
   trying to get across the creek,
    my sneakers
      slipping on the moss
as I poked around
   for a patch of gravel
    or sand to steady myself.
I fell over backwards,
   laughing and grasping at rocks
    as my body drifted rapidly
      and uncontrollably

downstream.

Back on dry land
   somewhat sobered
    I pondered . . .
Maybe I have terminal vertigo
   maybe I have a tumor on my brain
    maybe I won't live long
      maybe I'll get tremors.

Maybe I just have to adjust my medication.

GRANNY AND THE TREE

"Where have you been so long,
  Granny, my dear?" asked the tree.

"Down here, down here!"
  yelled Granny.

"Gravity's got me by the ankles,
  and I can't climb up no more."

Many years ago,
  when her eyes were clear,
  her back was strong,
  and she knew no fear

Granny'd built a bower
  high in the air
  of rough wooden planks,
  and a rope for a stair.

A mattress, too,
  and pillows everywhere,
  tapestried blankets,
  and a folding chair.

Content with her haven,
  she leaned her head
  on the boughs of the tree,
  where she made her bed.

And sang:

"I will gather berries,
hold them out between the leaves,
and the harbingers of summer
will fly to me—

and perch upon my finger,
as lightly as a breeze,
in the towering branches
of my Tree of Trees!"

Time had passed slowly
for the ancient oak,
two hundred years of solitude
and passing folk.

He ruled his leafy cousins
and his many protégés:
buckeye, dogwood, weeping willow,
maple, shining bay.

He was benevolent enough
(though haughty, some, and proud)
and liked a calm and simple life,
rooted to the ground.

So, he could not have conjured up
the loveliness and charm
of the girl who laughed and kissed him,
kept him safe from worldly harm,

who placed necklaces of pearls
and beads of glass around his limbs,
and in a voice as clear as silver
sang the tree her godly hymns.

But now . . .

"Time marches on," said he,
"nothing's here to stay."
And he shook his branches angrily
and turned his thoughts away.

Years ago, he promised her
he'd stand till she had gone,
till his trunk had turned to powder
and his spirit had withdrawn.

But looking down he saw her
with her hands upon his bark,
and humming softly to him,
was the splendid matriarch.

There within the moment
between heartbreak and release
came a dawning recognition
and to both an earthly peace.

She would reach one hundred
and he'd reach that times three,
but the legend would live longer yet
of Granny and the tree.

TOGETHER IN THE LIGHT IN THE DARKNESS

He was an absentee husband.

He loved my mother
desperately
fanatically
adoringly
blindly

but not well.

We kids gave him a thousand hints
of how he could make her happy

but there came no flowers
no symphony
no bistro
no pretty tea cup
no earrings.

He was instead
a great man
a fine teacher
a brilliant researcher
a doer of good deeds.

And now my mother carries the burden of guilt
"Why didn't I listen
when he told me about
the things
he loved:

math
physics
equations
standing waves?"

"Will you forgive me?"
she asks silently.
"Will you forgive me?"

She will walk back
again and again
into the utter chaos
of his house
out on the boardwalk
on the murky marsh.

And, in the midst of the
science weeklies
encyclopedias
awards for contributions to science
and humanitarian causes,

all the things
he cannot let go of,

in the midst of the clutter
she will move toward him
as he is crumbling
and she will breathe in
and breathe out
and touch him
his hand
his hurt knee
his forehead,

and they will be
together in the light
in the darkness.

INTO THE ETHER

Is *this* how the spirit feels
when it is already in the ether,
that it should go back and visit
all it ever knew?

The homes.
The pets.
The neighbors.
The school desks.

The slick grass.
The sturdy tree.
The perfect seashell.
The markers of my life.

Haven't I already marked them all?
And said a thousand goodbyes,
both casual and wrenching,
both empty and anguished?

I drift farther and farther from
the anxious faces that peer down at me.
They are offering some sunlight
when I am heading for the stars,

offering me sweet honey
when my tongue is long dead.

I have coasted past concern
for all of them,

past the aching pang for my son
past the security of my dogs,

whose heads would be resting
on my hips if only I could
lie on my side
and be rid of the pain.

But even the pain is fading now,
along with any concern for this body—
wracked or at ease,
it was only a husk all along.

Was that the dinner bell?
To put serum in my veins
and ashes in my mouth?
For what?

Another day of other people's
comings and goings,
their touching kindness,
their blunders, their fear?

I am drifting.

Is that the dinner bell?
Is this the chord I pull
if I need something?
But I don't need anything.

I drift.

The faces float,
the eyes reflect the pain

they think they see
in me.

But I am smiling.
I am closing my eyes.
I am counting backwards
from 100 . . .

96 . . .
93 . . .
80 . . .
71 . . .

I am in the schoolyard.
There's the metal carousel.
It's glinting! It's turning!
It's empty! How grand!

My turn!

The sun is dazzling.
I am running, slowly,
reaching to grab the shiny bar.
Where is everyone? No matter.

I grab.
I'm on!
I hold tight.
I lift off.

The sun is dazzling.
I'm spinning in the light.

WHEN YOU SEE MY MOTHER, ASK HER TO DANCE

for my mother and Jussi Björling (pronounced you-see)

On a dance floor somewhere
on the Eastern seaboard
in the summer of 1931,
a crowd of girls and almost-men.

In the cool shadows,
my teenage mother.
In the warm lights,
Swedish tenor Jussi Björling.

I courteously ask you, dear Jussi:
When you see my mother,
ask her to dance?

She's the dark girl.
She's a gypsy
and a vamp,
a foster child.
She's a flower.

She gazes up, her eyes
immense and frightened;
her lips are painted red
but sewn in silence.

Just behind a fluttering and
insufferable shyness, she thinks
(though no one ever says as much)
she might be beautiful.

You can tell her, Jussi!
She would hear the words from you,
this little bird adrift in flight
would hear the words from *you*.

She is but eighteen.
You are that plus two,
a prodigy,
a star already risen.

My mother is
too shy.
Your English
is too weak,

so, please extend your hand
accommodatingly and, with a smile,
lead her out, around, and through
the glittering crowd
and snapshot faces.

Grip my mother firmly by her waist
and to the surging strains
of violins,
bow just slightly,
and begin

to waltz.

You're light upon your feet, young man,
for one of such sturdy stock from
the land of ceaseless winters,

frozen lakes, and nights that
never end.

Your eyes are royal blue,
aquamarine or slate or powder;
they are Nordic sea-change eyes
set in your round and pleasant face,
deceptive in its jovial effect,
save for the force of an unyielding
jaw and chin—your armor in
the war
against the giving up of childhood.

In this ballroom, you are everything
to catch the eye,
handsome tux and fluted tie,
and now, my gypsy mother
by your side.

She moves with you in tandem,
leaning close against your mighty chest
with no more weight
than a small bird
alighting in its nest.

When she makes a move to leave
at song's end, keep her hand
and dance again, and then again,
until she's flushed and her vermillion lips
at last have parted in a smile.

So, then!

Guide her through the noisy coterie
and pour this girl a glass of punch.

How disarming is your presence
as you move tonight, Jussi!
Schooled in the opera at the age of four
toured with your brothers by the age of eight,
debuted with the Royal Swedish Opera at nineteen.

And so, in silence but with smiles
and whatever bond was born
of the dancing and the heat,
sip your drinks until they are
but melting bits of ice.

I ask you, dear Jussi, please take my mother
out onto the leafy balcony,
dappled dark and deserted.
Hear the click of her high heels
supporting slender legs and tender feet.

Do you see the concrete bench tucked in among the roses
over at the farthest end?
Notice the light of chandeliers and sconces
trapped inside the teeming hall
but casting muted rectangles,
which stretch as softly as the breeze
against the ivy covered walls?

The night cloaks my mother's
elegant little gown,
her elegant little gown
arranged for her by foster mothers,
all of whom meant well, I guess.

They took the Scottish waif
into the most prestigious stores in town,
and hinted to her,
coaxed her and suggested to her,
any pretty dress she might prefer.

Try as they might to pin her down,
she stood a frozen silhouette
against the shipwreck of her childhood,
where in all the ruins there was
not a shard of mirror to reflect her beauty
or show her some fine thing she might deserve.

So, the foster mothers did the choosing.
and though trying to be kind,
they tied fine lace and ribbons all around her,
and they tied her tongue at the same time.

And what of you, dear Jussi?
Your tongue quite clearly was not tied!
But whither went your childhood?
It was barely started when
at sixteen your mother died.

Had I been your mother
I would surely have been torn
between the grooming of a genius
and the countless ways that
childhood's careless days are formed.

Did she hear the timbre of your voice
the moment you were born?

Or in the summer breezes
you sing about and mourn?
Your voice resounds with
tears accumulated from the age of four,
when mystery's infant intuition
warned you of the coming hardships
you would certainly endure.

Out upon the darkened balcony,
My mother feels a rush of expectation
as she follows closely on your arm.

Hold her hand, dear Jussi,
lead her to the bench
and sit her down
and then: Sing to her!
Oh Jussi,
sing her anything!

In the ballroom, the orchestra
has just struck up some current hit
you know by heart,
and so, you sing to her—
you sit next to her,
hold her hand, and sing.

And as you sing, she feels
a quickening of her heart, a tingling
from head to toe—
or might it be from wing to wing?

Oh, dear Jussi, how your tux
lends splendor to the night!

It was your voice
that kept a pale ember burning
deep inside the guarded walls
beyond my mother's frozen silhouette.

So, out upon the balcony,
what happens next?

The song is over.
My mother's eyes shimmer
with a shock of tears,

with life.

The orchestra flips pages to another song.
You put your free hand
to my mother's cheek . . .
she is quite lovely, after all.

Her eyes close as she tilts her cheek into your wrist.

Does she clutch your hand?
Does she brush it with her lips?

When she meets your gaze again,
your sea-change eyes have imperceptibly
shifted to something like
surprise and curiosity,
an unsuspected wakening to
this half-seductive waif,
this shining bird,
this wild, heather-scented Scot.

What choice have you, dear Jussi,
but to kiss my mother!?
Kiss my mother!
Kiss her now,
before you even know her name,
or that your initials are the same:
Jussi Björling
Joan Bridge

It's but a soft embrace, a tender kiss.
My mother is not surprised, she is happy.

I make of this all that I please,
all that I wish, all I believe.

And I believe with all my heart and all my soul,

the filament that lines
the burnished edge of my own voice,
the naked talent I was given without choice,
that part of me
looks wistfully
and listens longingly
to songs sung on a balcony
a half a century
ago
my voice knows instinctively
it was conceived that night
in the dancing shadows,
in the dancing light.

As the years passed,
my mother remained

true to her dreams in black and white,
true to her youthful heart's delight.

And when she headed swiftly toward
the very edge of glory,
I pressed into her stubborn hand
a copy of this story—
a ticket, as it were,
to where sumptuous curtains
glide in silence
to reveal in living color
a familiar figure
on a stage . . .

And she stands,
a frozen silhouette
against the splendor of the present.

It's said the spirit has no fixed age
when it awakens to its change of circumstance.
But I think it is the age
of a certain moment
of exquisite chance.

So, when you see my mother,
ask her to dance!

WAVES

The last wave goodbye
is the first wave of acceptance.

ACKNOWLEDGMENTS

I wish to thank my coauthors B. B., Yasha, Star, The Raj, Frank, and Counsellor, as well as my coconspirators Joshua Bodwell, Nancy Lutzow, Thomas Lynch, Karen O'Connor, Beth Blachman, and Gabriele Rico.

A NOTE ABOUT THE AUTHOR

For more than six decades, Joan Baez has endured as a musical force of nature whose commitment to social activism has never wavered. Starting with her early 1960s recordings, she exerted a powerful attraction on a generation that sourced her traditional ballads for the rock vernacular, "House of the Rising Sun," "John Riley," "Jackaroe," "House Carpenter," and many more. She was inducted into the Rock & Roll Hall of Fame in 2017.

At the same time, Baez's role in the human rights and antiwar movements around the world has earned her place in history, alongside friends and allies including Dr. Martin Luther King Jr., Cesar Chavez, the Irish Peace People, Nelson Mandela, Vaclav Havel, and others.

Today, the life and times of Joan Baez are reflected in her "Mischief Makers" series of paintings that immortalize risk-taking visionaries ranging from Dr. King and Bob Dylan to the Dalai Lama and Patti Smith. In 2023, Godine published Baez's acclaimed book of drawings, *Am I Pretty When I Fly?*

A NOTE ON THE TYPE

When You See My Mother, Ask Her to Dance has been set in Aldus. Designed by Hermann Zapf and released by the German type foundry Stempel in 1954, Aldus is lighter and more refined than its family member Palatino, which is perhaps Zapf's most famous design. The popularity of Palatino after its release in 1949 led to its use in the body text of books, something Zapf had never intended for the display face. The elegant Aldus was his solution for book designers enamored by Palatino. Zapf's Optima has been used for titling.

Design & Composition by Tammy Ackerman